Animals and
Their Senses/
Los sentidos
de los animales

ANIMAL TOUCH/
EL TACTO EN LOS ANIMALES

by/por Kirsten Hall

Reading consultant/Consultora de lectura: Susan Nations, M.Ed.,
author, literacy coach, consultant/autora, tutora de alfabetización, consultora

WR WEEKLY
READER
EARLY LEARNING LIBRARY

Please visit our web site at: www.earlyliteracy.cc
For a free color catalog describing Weekly Reader® Early Learning Library's list
of high-quality books, call 1-877-445-5824 (USA) or 1-800-387-3178 (Canada).
Weekly Reader® Early Learning Library's fax: (414) 336-0164.

Library of Congress Cataloging-in-Publication Data available upon request from the publisher.
Fax (414) 336-0157 for the attention of the Publishing Records Department.

ISBN 0-8368-4818-7 (lib. bdg.)
ISBN 0-8368-4824-1 (softcover)

This North American edition first published in 2006 by
Weekly Reader® Early Learning Library
A Member of the WRC Media Family of Companies
330 West Olive Street, Suite 100
Milwaukee, WI 53212 USA

Copyright © 2006 by Nancy Hall, Inc.
Spanish text copyright © 2006 by Weekly Reader® Early Learning Library

Weekly Reader® Early Learning Library Editor: Barbara Kiely Miller
Weekly Reader® Early Learning Library Art Direction: Tammy West
Weekly Reader® Early Learning Library Graphic Designer and Page Layout: Jenni Gaylord
Weekly Reader® Early Learning Library Translators: Tatiana Acosta and Guillermo Gutiérrez

Photo Credits
The publisher would like to thank the following for permission to reproduce their royalty-free photographs:
AbleStock: 8, 17, 18; Brand X Pictures: 19; Corel: 21; Digital Vision: cover, title page, 6, 7, 12, 13, 16;
EyeWire: 9; Fotosearch/Brand X Pictures: 20; Fotosearch/Corbis: 4, 10; Fotosearch/Digital Vision: 15;
Fotosearch/Goodshoot: 11; Fotosearch/image 100: 5; Fotosearch/SuperStock: 14

Printed in the United States of America

1 2 3 4 5 6 7 8 9 09 08 07 06 05

Note to Educators and Parents

Reading is such an exciting adventure for young children! They are beginning to integrate their oral language skills with written language. To encourage children along the path to early literacy, books must be colorful, engaging, and interesting; they should invite the young reader to explore both the print and the pictures.

Animals and Their Senses is a new series designed to help children read about the five senses in animals. In each book young readers will learn interesting facts about the bodies of some animals and how the featured sense works for them.

Each book is specially designed to support the young reader in the reading process. The familiar topics are appealing to young children and invite them to read — and reread — again and again. The full-color photographs and enhanced text further support the student during the reading process.

In addition to serving as wonderful picture books in schools, libraries, homes, and other places where children learn to love reading, these books are specifically intended to be read within an instructional guided reading group. This small group setting allows beginning readers to work with a fluent adult model as they make meaning from the text. After children develop fluency with the text and content, the book can be read independently. Children and adults alike will find these books supportive, engaging, and fun!

— Susan Nations, M.Ed., author/literacy coach/reading consultant

Nota para los educadores y los padres

¡Leer es una aventura tan emocionante para los niños pequeños! A esta edad están comenzando a integrar su manejo del lenguaje oral con el lenguaje escrito. Para animar a los niños en el camino de la lectura incipiente, los libros deben ser coloridos, estimulantes e interesantes; deben invitar a los jóvenes lectores a explorar la letra impresa y las ilustraciones.

Los sentidos de los animales es una nueva colección diseñada para que los niños lean textos sobre los cinco sentidos en los animales. En cada libro, los jóvenes lectores aprenderán datos interesantes del cuerpo de algunos animales y cómo éstos usan el sentido que se presenta.

Cada libro está especialmente diseñado para ayudar a los jóvenes lectores en el proceso de lectura. Los temas familiares llaman la atención de los niños y los invitan a leer — y releer — una y otra vez. Las fotografías a todo color y el tamaño de la letra ayudan aún más al estudiante en el proceso de lectura.

Además de servir como maravillosos libros ilustrados en escuelas, bibliotecas, hogares y otros lugares donde los niños aprenden a amar la lectura, estos libros han sido especialmente concebidos para ser leídos en un grupo de lectura guiada. Este contexto permite que los lectores incipientes trabajen con un adulto que domina la lectura mientras van determinando el significado del texto. Una vez que los niños dominan el texto y el contenido, el libro puede ser leído de manera independiente. ¡Estos libros les resultarán útiles, estimulantes y divertidos a niños y a adultos por igual!

— Susan Nations, M.Ed., autora/tutora de alfabetización/consultora de desarrollo de la lectura

People touch with their skin. **Nerves** in our skin carry information about what we touch to our brains.

- - - - - - - -

Las personas tenemos el sentido del tacto en la piel. **Nervios** en nuestra piel llevan al cerebro información acerca de lo que tocamos.

The tips of our fingers have many **nerve endings**. They help us know whether something is hard or soft, hot or cold, smooth or bumpy, or wet or dry.

- - - - - - - -

Las puntas de nuestros dedos tienen muchas **terminaciones nerviosas**. Éstas nos ayudan a saber si algo es duro o blando, liso o rugoso, si está caliente o frío, mojado o seco.

A raccoon's front paws have thousands more nerve endings than human fingers do. Raccoons can find food in the dark or underwater just by touching it.

‒ ‒ ‒ ‒ ‒ ‒ ‒ ‒

Las zarpas delanteras del mapache tienen miles de terminaciones nerviosas más que los dedos humanos. Los mapaches pueden encontrar alimento en la oscuridad o debajo del agua usando sólo el tacto.

Most frogs have a very good sense of touch. Frogs feel objects with their fingertips, too.

- - - - - - - - -

La mayoría de las ranas tiene un sentido del tacto muy sensible. Las ranas perciben con la punta de los dedos cómo son las cosas al tacto.

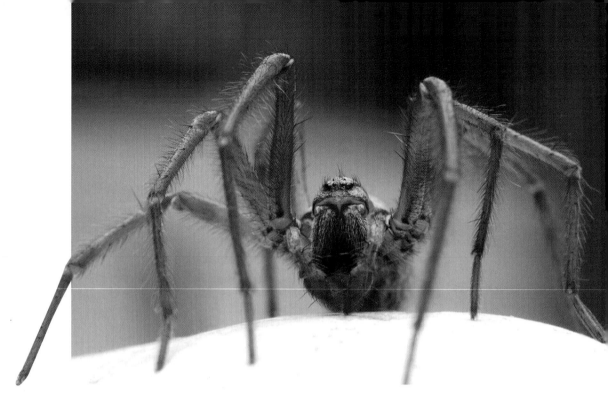

A spider has small hairs on its eight legs. The hairs help a spider feel objects move and movements in the air when **prey** is nearby.

- - - - - - - -

La araña tiene pequeños pelos en sus ocho patas. Cuando su **presa** está cerca, estos pelillos la ayudan a percibir si algo se mueve o si el aire vibra.

whiskers/bigotes

The long stiff hairs on a seal's face, called whiskers, can feel movements in the water. The **whiskers** help the seal catch fish even when the water is dark.

— — — — — — — —

Los pelos largos y duros, llamados **bigotes**, de la cara de la foca pueden percibir si algo se mueve en el agua. Los bigotes ayudan a la foca a atrapar peces aun cuando el agua está oscura.

Cats use their whiskers like feelers. Whiskers help cats know when objects are close to them, especially in the dark.

— — — — — — — —

Los felinos usan sus bigotes como antenas. Los bigotes ayudan a los felinos a saber si tienen algo cerca, especialmente en la oscuridad.

tentacle/tentáculo

Snails use their bottom **tentacles** to feel their way around. They also use these tentacles to taste and smell.

▬ ▬ ▬ ▬ ▬ ▬ ▬ ▬ ▬

Los caracoles usan los **tentáculos** que tienen por debajo para tantear el camino. También usan estos tentáculos para percibir sabores y olores.

trunk/trompa

Some animals touch each other to say hello. Elephants greet each other by rubbing their trunks together.

- - - - - - - -

Algunos animales se tocan unos a otros para saludarse. Los elefantes frotan entre sí sus trompas.

Some animals touch each other to be helpful. Monkeys use their fingers to clean each other's fur.

— — — — — — — —

Algunos animales se tocan unos a otros para ayudarse. Los monos se limpian el pelaje unos a otros con los dedos.

Many animals use touch to show caring. Giraffes show caring by touching each other's noses.

— — — — — — — — —

Muchos animales usan el tacto para demostrar cariño. Las jirafas se tocan el hocico unas a otras para demostrar afecto.

Sometimes touching can hurt! Kangaroos hit and kick each
other when they are fighting.

- - - - - - - -

¡Hay formas de tocar que duelen! Los canguros se pegan y se
patean cuando están peleando.

Polar bears sit, walk, and sleep on snow and ice. A polar bear's body is covered with thick fur that helps keep the bear from feeling the cold.

Los osos polares se sientan, caminan y duermen sobre la nieve y el hielo. Sus cuerpos están cubiertos de un pelaje grueso que los ayuda a no sentir el frío.

Penguins swim in cold water and walk on ice and snow. A penguin's body has a thick layer of **blubber**, or fat, that helps keep it warm.

- - - - - - - -

Los pingüinos nadan en aguas frías y caminan sobre el hielo y la nieve. Sus cuerpos tienen una gruesa capa de grasa que los ayuda a no pasar frío.

Many animals live in very hot places. Desert lizards have long legs that help keep their bodies from touching the hot sand and rocks.

- - - - - - - -

Muchos animales viven en lugares muy calurosos. Los lagartos del desierto tienen las patas largas para que sus cuerpos no toquen la arena y las piedras calientes.

A camel's knees, elbows, and chest have pads of thick skin.
The pads let the camel lie down on the hot sand.

■ ■ ■ ■ ■ ■ ■ ■ ■

Las rodillas, los codos y el pecho del camello están recubiertos
de piel muy gruesa. Gracias a eso, el camello puede echarse
en la arena caliente.

Orangutans use touch to comfort their young. A young orangutan stays with its mother for seven or eight years.

— — — — — — — —

Los orangutanes usan el sentido del tacto para consolar a sus crías. Una cría de orangután se queda con su madre entre siete y ocho años.

Animals use their sense of touch in many ways. Touch helps
an animal learn about where it lives.

■ ■ ■ ■ ■ ■ ■ ■ ■

Los animales usan su sentido del tacto de muchas maneras. El
tacto ayuda a los animales a conocer el lugar donde viven.

Glossary

nerve endings — the tips of nerves

nerves — thin, stringlike parts that carry messages between the brain and other parts of the body

prey— animals that are hunted and killed by other animals for food

tentacles — long, bendable parts that stick out from the heads of some animals

Glosario

nervios — cordones delgados que transportan los mensajes entre el cerebro y las demás partes del cuerpo

presa — animal que otros animales cazan para alimentarse

tentáculos — partes largas y flexibles que sobresalen de la cabeza de algunos animales

terminaciones nerviosas — puntas de los nervios

For More Information/Más información

Books

Amazing Animals. Rookie Reader (series).
Betsy Franco (Scholastic)

Animal Senses: How Animals See, Hear, Taste, Smell and Feel. Pamela Hickman (Kids Can Press)

Libros

Giraffes/Los jirafas. Animals I See at the Zoo/
Animales que veo en el zoológico (series).
JoAnn Early Macken (Weekly Reader Early Learning Library)

El canguro. Animales del zoológico (series).
Patricia Whitehouse (Heinemann Library)

Index

Índice

About the Author

Kirsten Hall is an author and editor. While she was still in high school, she published her first book for children, *Bunny, Bunny*. Since then she has written and published more than eighty titles. A former teacher, Kirsten currently spends her days writing and editing and her evenings tutoring. She lives in New York City with her husband.

Información sobre la autora

Kirsten Hall es escritora y editora. Publicó su primer libro para niños, *Bunny, Bunny*, cuando aún asistía a la escuela secundaria. Desde entonces, ha escrito y publicado más de ochenta títulos. Kirsten, que anteriormente fue maestra, pasa el día escribiendo y editando, y por la noche da clases. Kirsten vive en la ciudad de Nueva York con su esposo.